W9-BXF-952

Police Dogs

Dog Tales:
True Stories About Amazing Dogs

Dog Tales:
True Stories About Amazing Dogs

Police Dogs

Marie-Therese Miller

CHELSEA
CLUBHOUSE
An Imprint of Chelsea House Publishers

Police Dogs

© 2007 by Infobase Publishing

All rights reserved. No part of this book may be reproduced or utilized in any form or by any means, electronic or mechanical, including photocopying, recording, or by any information storage or retrieval systems, without permission in writing from the publisher. For information contact:

Chelsea Clubhouse
An imprint of Infobase Publishing
132 West 31st Street
New York, NY 10001

ISBN-10: 0-7910-9036-1
ISBN-13: 978-0-7910-9036-7

Library of Congress Cataloging-in-Publication Data
Miller, Marie-Therese.
    Police dogs / Marie-Therese Miller.
        p. cm. — (Dog tales)
    Includes bibliographical references and index.
    ISBN 0-7910-9036-1 (hardcover)
    1. Police dogs—United States—Juvenile literature. 2. Police dogs—
New York—Dutchess County—Juvenile literature. I. Title. II. Series.
    HV8025.M55 2007
    363.28—dc22   2006024081

Chelsea House and Chelsea Clubhouse books are available at special discounts when purchased in bulk quantities for businesses, associations, institutions, or sales promotions. Please call our Special Sales Department in New York at (212) 967-8800 or (800) 322-8755.

You can find Chelsea House and Chelsea Clubhouse on the World Wide Web at http://www.chelseahouse.com

Development Editor: Anna Prokos
Text Design: Annie O'Donnell
Cover Design: Ben Peterson

Printed in the United States of America

Bang FOF 10 9 8 7 6 5 4 3 2 1

This book is printed on acid-free paper.

All links and Web addresses were checked and verified to be correct at the time of publication. Because of the dynamic nature of the Web, some addresses and links may have changed since publication and may no longer be valid.

Contents

Police Partners

Bojar is always ready for action. As a trained police dog, this male German shepherd is prepared when his police partner needs him. Sergeant Frank LaMonica is Bojar's partner. The two work for the Dutchess County Sheriff's Office in New York State. Bojar helps in many aspects of law enforcement work. He can catch criminals, find missing people, protect innocent citizens, patrol the streets, and much more. Bojar and Sgt. LaMonica are partners, and both of their jobs are equally important.

Because *canine* is another word for *dog*, police dogs are called K-9s. Like many other police dogs, K-9 Bojar was born in Slovakia in Europe. Many police officers acquire their patrol dogs from European breeders. That's because these breeders specialize in producing working dogs as well as canines that can compete in the sport of **Schutzhund**. *Schutzhund* is a German word that means protection dog. The sport tests the dog's ability to protect, obey, and track. All of these are vital skills for good police dogs.

CHOOSING A PARTNER

Police officers are very involved in choosing the right dog to be their K-9 partner. They pick their young dogs using a **temperament** evaluation. This test will demonstrate if the dog has the potential to become a successful police dog. First, a police officer may throw a toy into tall grass. He's looking for a dog with a strong drive to search for the toy until it is found. This is a good indicator that the dog can be trained to locate people and evidence. In addition, police dogs are rewarded with play, so an officer wants a dog that loves a game of fetch or tug of war.

Next, the officer may wear a padded sleeve, known as a bite sleeve, and approach the dog in a threatening way. A dog that defends itself, and doesn't cower or run away, shows that it can effectively chase or stop criminals and also protect its partner.

Sgt. Frank LaMonica and Bojar, his trained German shepherd police dog, work together at the Dutchess County Sheriff's Office in New York State. The police partners help track criminals, protect the community, and much more.

Police officers are very involved in choosing the right dog to be their K-9 partner. Officers look for certain traits that show the young dog can be a successful police K-9.

One-year-old Bojar did well in his evaluation, so Sgt. LaMonica chose Bojar and began the hard work required to train a police dog. Bojar is a dual-purpose canine. He works as a patrol dog and accompanies Sgt. LaMonica to help with police work each day. But Bojar is also a **cadaver** detection dog, which means he uses his keen sense of smell to locate dead bodies.

INTENSE TRAINING

For the first step in training, Bojar needed to learn patrol dog duties. He attended an 11-week patrol dog school with Sgt. LaMonica. There, Bojar was taught to respond to obedience commands. Why is obedience the first step in training? A patrol dog must be extremely obedient and listen to the commands of his police handler. If his handler tells him to stop a criminal who is holding a gun, for example, the dog must act without hesitation.

Sgt. LaMonica issues commands to Bojar in Slovak. Many police officers give their K-9s commands

Police dogs have to climb fences, jump through open windows, and be quick on their feet. Obstacle courses are physically demanding in order to keep police dogs agile for the situations they might face while at work.

in the dog's native language because the young dog is familiar with the words used in his homeland. Plus, the special language between police officer and police dog makes it less likely that anyone else could command the dog. In addition, commands given in a foreign language can confuse a criminal. A criminal who doesn't know if the K-9 is being ordered to sit or attack might be more easily convinced to surrender.

During training, Bojar learned to respond to both verbal commands and accompanying hand signals. The silent hand signals are useful when the police officer doesn't want a criminal to hear where he and his K-9 are located. The officer must be able to silently command his dog to come or stay without warning the criminal.

Because police dogs often have to climb fences, jump through open windows, or leap from patrol cars, part of their training requires **agility** work. While at patrol school, Bojar spent some time navigating an obstacle course. He walked across narrow beams and through large, round pipes. He made his way up and down ladders and wooden slopes. These physically demanding courses keep police dogs agile and ready for real-life obstacles they might encounter while at work.

In addition to being agile, a patrol dog must be physically strong, lean, and healthy. Sgt. LaMonica

BELGIAN MALINOIS VS. GERMAN SHEPHERD

Many police departments choose large, muscular dogs, such as Belgian Malinois and German shepherds, to help with law enforcement work. It can be easy to confuse these two dog breeds because they have a similar appearance. There are differences, however, that you can spot.

The Belgian Malinois is a variety of Belgian shepherd. It is smaller boned than the German shepherd, has a more chiseled face, and equilateral triangle-shaped ears. A Belgian Malinois seems to walk on its toes, while the German shepherd moves on a flatter foot.

Because a German shepherd is usually longer than it is tall, it looks rectangular from the side. The Belgian Malinois' length is nearly equal to its height, so it looks more like a square. The German shepherd's back area slopes downward from its shoulders to its tail, but the Belgian Malinois doesn't have as pronounced a slope.

The coat of the Belgian Malinois is often an overall fawn color with a black section of fur on the face that looks like a mask.

(continues)

German shepherds (left) and Belgian Malinois are popular police dogs that have several differences.

(continued)

The German shepherd's fur is commonly darker on the torso and appears saddle-like.

Police officers know that Belgian Malinois and German shepherds have ideal qualities for police work. Both breeds are known to be intelligent, energetic, and protective. No matter how they differ in appearance, they both make superior police dogs.

couldn't have a flabby K-9 trying to keep up with a fleeing criminal. Therefore, Bojar was not rewarded for his correct behavior with dog treats. Instead, Sgt. LaMonica gave him verbal praise, petting, and play-time with a favorite toy as rewards for good performance. Once his obedience and agility were proven, Bojar was ready to learn his aggression, protection, and scenting skills.

Learning Aggression and Scent Work

With police cars hot on the tail of a fleeing car, a criminal jumps from the automobile and makes a quick escape into the woods. A patrol dog needs to be able to race after the criminal, find him, and hold him until a police officer can make the arrest. If the criminal physically threatens the police officer, the dog must act to protect its handler. During patrol school, Bojar learned aggression, protection, and scenting skills so he could perform his job well.

First, Bojar learned how to bite and hold the class instructor, who pretended to be a "bad" guy. In early training, the instructor would wear a bite sleeve. As training progressed, the instructor wore a full bite suit made of cushioned material that covers the arms, legs, and torso. While the instructor pretended to be a criminal, Sgt. LaMonica commanded Bojar to go after the **decoy**. Bojar was taught to bite the instructor once and hold fast until Sgt. LaMonica ordered the K-9 to release the bad guy.

Next, Bojar learned the specific command to bark and hold. Sgt. LaMonica's command sent Bojar racing toward the instructor, who was wearing the bite-suit. Bojar barked menacingly at him. With the bark and hold, the dog is not permitted to bite unless the bad guy tries to run or physically threatens the K-9 or his handler. The bark and hold requires serious self-control on the part of the patrol dog. One very complicated lesson that Bojar had to master was to stop a bark and hold and return to his handler, who was standing a distance away. This is an especially tricky task if the decoy begins to run because a K-9's natural instinct is to chase prey.

During patrol school, Bojar was also taught handler protection. The only time a patrol dog is permitted to act without a command is when his handler is in danger.

New York Department of Environmental Protection Police Officer Greg Marinelli wears a bite sleeve, which helps train police dogs to bite criminals upon their police partners' commands.

Dutchess County Sheriff's Office Sgt. Frank LaMonica explains how the bite suit protects Town of Poughkeepsie Police Officer Mike Burger, the decoy criminal. Bite suits are made of thick, cushioned material that keeps the officer safe from K-9 teeth during training and demonstrations.

SCENT WORK

Another important part of a patrol dog's job is to locate criminals and find evidence. Bojar was taught to use his keen sense of smell to perform these critical tasks. German shepherds have about 220 million **olfactory sensory cells**, which help the dogs gather and process scents. Human beings only have approximately 5 million of these cells. By using his naturally keen scenting ability, Bojar learned to detect and track scents.

How do K-9s use their superior scenting skills to find people? Human beings shed approximately 40,000 dead skin cells each minute. These dead skin cells are known as **rafts**. Dogs can smell these rafts and follow them to the place where the human scent is strongest. That's usually where the person is located.

At patrol school, Bojar learned to perform building and area searches. Bojar used his sharp nose to gather scent from the air and follow it. This canine skill is called **air scenting**. During training, Bojar used his air scenting ability to find a person hidden in a building, such as a warehouse, or a secluded area, such as a field.

Bojar also was taught to do article searches to find items that had been handled by a person. Because human beings leave scent on objects that they touch, Bojar could use his nose to locate those things. He would be able to help Sgt. LaMonica search for knives or guns that were used in a crime, or for stolen goods, such as jewelry, that may have been handled by a criminal. Whatever Bojar would find during real-life police scenarios could later be used as evidence to convict the criminal.

Police dogs are called upon to find criminals who are running from the police, lost children, or disoriented people. In patrol school, Bojar learned to do this by tracking, or following a scent trail that's left on the ground.

To teach Bojar how to track, the instructor laid a scent track by walking through an area. Sgt. LaMonica placed Bojar in a harness and attached a long leash known as a **tracking line**. Sgt. LaMonica brought Bojar near the point where the instructor began laying the trail. Then, Bojar used his nose to track the instructor's rafts. The crushed grass, leaves, and plants that the instructor had stepped on also left a scent for Bojar to follow.

After Bojar had some practice tracking, Sgt. LaMonica taught him to begin the track by smelling a scent article, an item that carries a particular person's odor. Sgt. LaMonica had Bojar sniff the instructor's hat. Bojar was then able to find the beginning of the track with his sense of smell, and the hunt began.

THE K-9 CAR

How can a specially equipped police car help K-9s like Bojar protect their human police partners? Imagine that Sgt. LaMonica stops a vehicle to issue a ticket. He leaves Bojar in the back seat and approaches the other automobile. The driver jumps out, wielding a knife in her hand. Sgt. LaMonica needs Bojar's help, so he uses a special remote control to pop open the back door of the police car. Bojar bolts from the car, tackles the armed driver, and saves Sgt. LaMonica.

K-9 police cars, such as this one used by the Dutchess County Sheriff's Office, are often equipped to handle the needs and comforts of police dogs.

The police cruisers that the Dutchess County Sheriff's Office uses have other features that cater to the K-9 team. While Sgt. LaMonica drives a K-9 car, Bojar is comfortable in an area built especially for him. In most K-9 vehicles, the back seat has been removed and replaced with a large aluminum kennel to house large police dogs.

In addition, Sgt. LaMonica doesn't have to worry about leaving Bojar alone in the police car, even in the heat of summer. The car has sensors that roll down the windows and sound an alarm when the temperature in the automobile becomes too high.

The specially designed K-9 police car helps make daily patrol work safer for both the police officer and the skilled police canine.

DETECTION DUTY

After patrol school, dual-purpose K-9s like Bojar also attend detector school, which lasts about six weeks. Detector dogs are taught to find specific materials, and they use their super-sensitive noses to do it. Sgt. LaMonica offers this analogy to explain a detector dog's sharp scenting ability: "I know that my wife is cooking spaghetti sauce. Bojar would know what ingredients, like oregano, are in the sauce."

Detector dogs can be trained to home in on particular scents. Narcotic detection dogs, for example, are trained to find illegal drugs. Other police dogs work as explosive detector K-9s, using their scenting skills to detect the materials used to make bombs. Bojar took private lessons in cadaver detection, so he was taught to find human remains in places such as forests, trunks of cars, or even bodies of water.

With all of his schooling behind him, Bojar was ready to apply his new, hard-earned skills as he worked alongside Sgt. LaMonica.

Bojar on the Job

Bojar and Sgt. LaMonica work the late afternoon into the night shift for the Dutchess County Sheriff's Office in New York State. During their workday, the pair utilizes the skills they acquired at school. They locate and apprehend criminals and recover weapons and stolen property. Bojar and Sgt. LaMonica are needed for other important duties as well.

One night in particular, Sgt. LaMonica and Bojar were called to a scene outside a restaurant. A large crowd of people had gathered, and they had become very agitated. Sgt. LaMonica placed Bojar on a leash, and the two walked toward the group. Just the sight of the police officer and his imposing K-9 calmed the crowd. Soon, every individual went his or her separate way.

During the course of a day, Bojar and Sgt. LaMonica can be contacted to track criminals who are attempting to escape capture. They may also be called to help find children or disoriented adults who

K-9 units often meet for training sessions to sharpen the skills that the dogs and handlers learned at patrol school.

have become lost. Sgt. LaMonica told a funny story about a K-9 unit that was called to search for a child. The police dog was given the child's pillowcase to sniff. Then, the dog began to track. He tracked the child directly into the family's house and to a closet, where the child had fallen asleep, hidden from her parent's view. There's never a dull moment in the life of a police dog!

PRACTICE, PRACTICE, PRACTICE

In addition to the long hours Sgt. LaMonica and Bojar spend patrolling Dutchess County, they meet regularly with other K-9 units for training sessions. During patrol training, the skills that the dogs and handlers learned at patrol school are sharpened.

Patrol training days often include tracking. The dogs practice tracking in all types of weather conditions. They track in snow, rain, and in the heat of summer. A police officer lays a scent track by weaving across a farmer's field, where horses and cows normally graze. The scent track may snake into the woods, across creeks, and even change direction. The track holds many challenges for Bojar and the other practicing K-9s because it has the added scents of the animals that graze in the field. Also, following smells through water and changes in direction can be tricky.

Sgt. LaMonica and Bojar usually wait about two hours before tackling the scent track. The older the track, the more difficult it is to follow the scent.

K-9 MAX AND SGT. LAMONICA

Before K-9 Bojar and Sgt. LaMonica became a Dutchess County Sheriff's Office team, Sgt. LaMonica was partnered with a German shepherd dog named Max. Max was born in the Czech Republic. He was a dual-purpose K-9, trained as a patrol dog and as a narcotics detection canine.

Max and Sgt. LaMonica were on the job together for nine years. During that time, they captured many criminals and helped count-less citizens. Sgt. LaMonica recalled two instances in particular. One time, he and Max were tracking two juvenile burglars who fell into a creek. The teens struggled out of the water and continued to run in the below-freezing weather. Fortunately, Max was able to find them before they suffered from hypothermia.

Another time, a young woman had hidden deep in the woods and attempted to kill herself by taking too many pills. Max tracked her quickly, and the partners took her for emergency medical help. Max and Sgt. LaMonica saved her life.

Finally, the time came for Max to retire from police work. At a certain point, a police dog becomes too old to perform his duties because he doesn't have the stamina or agility that is needed.

In Max.'s retirement, he continued to live with Sgt. LaMonica and his family. It was difficult for Max to give up police work. "Retire-ment was really hard for him. When the phone rang in the middle of the night, he was ready to go," said Sgt. LaMonica.

Max died in the spring of 2005. His death was a great loss to the Dutchess County community and, most of all, to Sgt. LaMonica. "He was a good partner, and my best friend," said Sgt. LaMonica.

Sgt. LaMonica places Bojar in his harness and tracking line and leads him to an area close to where the police officer began laying the track. Bojar must locate the exact place the track starts. He puts his nose down and sniffs. Soon, he's off and running. After completing the complex track, Bojar is rewarded; the police officer who laid the track waits to congratulate the successful canine.

AFTER HOURS

After regular work hours, Sgt. LaMonica and Bojar continue to train. They often go to local playgrounds to keep Bojar agile. Bojar climbs jungle gym bars and balances on seesaws.

Sgt. LaMonica also takes Bojar to shopping malls in order to expose him to the marble flooring in the building. They go on walks across icy pavement. A police dog needs to keep his footing no matter what substance is under his paws.

The pair also visits schools so that students can understand the police officer and K-9 team. Sgt. LaMonica demonstrates Bojar's ability to climb and jump. He lets the children see how well Bojar responds to commands. Sgt. LaMonica also chooses one student to take small toy and hide it anywhere on the school grounds. Then Bojar demonstrates his article search ability. He uses his keen nose to locate the item in minutes.

Whatever their day holds, Bojar always goes home to live with Sgt. LaMonica and his family. The dog loves to jump on the couch and cuddle,

During a community demonstration, Sgt. Frank LaMonica permits Caroline Kiernan, a student at Joseph D'Aquanni West Road Intermediate School, to pet his K-9 partner, Bojar. Bojar and LaMonica often travel to Dutchess County, NY, schools so that kids can learn about the important work of police dogs in a community.

DETECTING THE DEAD

A person has been murdered, but no body has been located. Bojar and Dutchess County Sheriff's Officer Sgt. LaMonica are asked to help. Bojar is a cadaver detection dog, which means he can find dead human bodies using his keen sense of smell.

Sgt. LaMonica orders Bojar to sniff around the murder suspect's car because sometimes murder victims are hidden in vehicle trunks. They search the wooded acres behind the murder suspect's home. When Bojar gives his aggressive alert, scratching, the body he discovers can be used as evidence in the crime.

To learn to find human remains, Bojar and Sgt. LaMonica attended a private cadaver detection class. The method used to teach Bojar to find and alert to human remains was similar to narcotics detection training, except that the scent used in Bojar's schooling was decomposed human odor.

After Bojar mastered the basic detector skills, Sgt. LaMonica continued training him on more complicated problems. Sgt. LaMonica would bury human remains scent deep into the woods and leave it for one entire month. Then, he would challenge Bojar to locate it. Bojar is so well trained that he will ignore the smell of other dead animals and only alert his handler to the scent of a dead *human*. Plus, under some conditions, Bojar can locate a drowned body under 100 feet (30.5 m) of water.

Bojar and Sgt. LaMonica also help out in cases of accidental death. They are contacted to find people who have drowned or have been missing in the wilderness for a long time and are presumed dead. When Bojar finds human remains, he gives the victim's family peace of mind. Although the family feels sad about the death, they are usually relieved to know what happened to their loved one and to be able to plan a funeral service and burial.

but he never rests for long. He's always ready to go to work whenever his special police dog skills are needed.

Detecting Explosives

A man enters an electronics store at the Hudson Valley Mall near Kingston, New York. He opens fire with an automatic weapon. Tragically, he wounds two shoppers before three brave mall employees wrestle him to the floor. Area police forces are called to the crime scene.

The responding police agencies have spotted a suspicious car parked near a sporting goods store at the mall. They are worried that it might contain explosives. Sometimes, criminals plant a bomb timed

Police officer Greg Marinelli and Niko, a patrol K-9 that is also trained in explosive detection, maintain their police work skills at frequent training sessions. The team works for the New York City Department of Environmental Protection Police Department.

to blow up when all the police and fire departments are at the crime scene. This is called a secondary device.

An alert goes out for the New York City Department of Environmental Protection (DEP) police K-9 units. DEP police officer Greg Marinelli and his police dog, Niko, respond. Niko, a Belgian Malinois, is both a patrol K-9 and an explosive detection dog.

When they arrive at the mall scene, Officer Marinelli leads Niko to the suspicious vehicle. If Niko smells explosives, he will sit where he detects the distinct odor. This is called a passive alert. Explosive detection dogs do not learn to scratch or bark near bombs because that may cause an explosion.

Niko sniffs around the car's tires and bumpers. He checks under the seats and on the dashboard. Fortunately, he does not detect any explosives. But Officer Marinelli and Niko are just beginning their long night of work. They enter the mall and search every single store and each area of the building. No bomb is found.

New York Department of Environmental Protection Police Officer Greg Marinelli watches as an officer-in-training works with her K-9.

Because Niko is also a patrol dog, Officer Marinelli uses him to search the mall for other criminals, in case the shooter was not acting alone. In addition, Niko looks for people who may have been injured. He locates store owners and customers who may have gone into hiding during the shooting. Police officers escort the people Niko finds to safety.

Niko and his handler worked this particular scene for nine hours to make certain that the mall was safe. They succeeded in protecting the civilians and fellow officers in the area.

EXPLOSIVE DETECTION SCHOOL

How did Niko learn his amazing bomb finding skills? Like Bojar, Niko attended the 11-week patrol school with Officer Marinelli. Niko learned to perform most of the patrol canine duties, but instructors did not teach him to pick up weapons or stolen goods during article searches. It would be extremely dangerous for an explosive detection dog to retrieve a pipe bomb with his teeth.

Following patrol school, Officer Marinelli and Niko went to a six-week explosive detection course. There, Niko learned to identify eight explosive scents: nitrate, black powder, smokeless powder, TNT, C4, dynamite, Royal Demolition Explosive (RMX), and High Melting Point Explosive (HMX).

Explosive detection dogs and their handlers attend training exercises, such as this one conducted at the Naval Station in San Diego. Master at Arms Second Class Kirk Kuchenreuther and his dog Kazan search for explosive material hidden in office shelving.

All eight explosives were placed in a wooden box with a hole in the lid. The combination of scents provided the canines with a strong, unmistakable explosive odor. That box was put in a line with four or five other similar containers, which did not contain the scents.

Officer Marinelli walked Niko beside the boxes and had him sniff each one. "Check," he commanded. When Niko reached the scented box, he was instructed in Czechoslovakian to "sit." Then, one by one, the explosive scents were removed from the box, until Niko could recognize each individual odor.

When Niko learned to sit at the proper container, he was given his favorite toy. Officer Marinelli

PROTECTING THE ENVIRONMENT

The New York City Department of Environmental Protection (DEP) Police K-9 units, like Officer Greg Marinelli and Niko, play an important part in keeping the city safe. The DEP is responsible for protecting the watersheds, which means they make sure the water supply is clean and healthy for drinking. To do this, the DEP police patrol the upstate reservoirs, dams, and water facilities.

Niko and Officer Marinelli are always on the look out for suspicious strangers who might try to contaminate the water supply or for bombers who might use explosives to target dams.

In addition, if other police departments in the area need the services of an explosive detection dog, the DEP will loan Officer Marinelli and Niko to them. Sometimes, Niko is asked to perform

would also holler "good boy" and pet Niko. The dogs are rewarded with a combination of play and praise to enforce the lessons.

Mike Burger, a police officer for the Town of Pough-keepsie in New York, is also K-9 trainer who works alongside the Dutchess County Sheriff's Office. "You have to be goofy and fun with the dog and not be worried about embarrassment," he explains, regarding the police K-9 reward system.

KEEPING K-9 NOSES SHARP

Officer Marinelli and Niko are constantly practicing detection skills. At least twice a week, Officer Marinelli hides bomb scents for his canine to seek. Once a

advanced security details for high profile individuals visiting the city. Not long ago, Officer Marinelli and Niko searched an auditorium where New York Senator Hillary Clinton was scheduled to speak. Niko checked under the seats and along the stage to be certain that everyone would be safe.

Another time the police pair was called into action was when police officers stopped a suspicious box truck that was traveling an upstate New York highway. Officer Marinelli and Niko were asked to search for explosives in that vehicle. Niko used his well-trained nose to sniff the truck's cab and cargo area. The New York City DEP police K-9 units are busy keeping the water safe for city residents, but they are never too busy to help other police agencies in need.

month, they travel to train with the Dutchess County Sheriff's Office K-9 units.

These detector-training sessions are held at varied locations to test the dogs' skills in many environments. One month, they might train in a dark, abandoned mall; the next session might be held in small hotel rooms. The trainers tuck small amounts of explosive scent in tricky locations, such as heating vents or behind thermostats, to truly challenge the canines and their handlers.

Just how sensitive are the noses of explosive detection dogs? During one training session, a bomb K-9 gave a passive alert at a motel room wall with a small crack in the plaster. The hidden explosives were actually on the other side of the wall in the next motel room!

ON THE JOB

Explosive detection dogs and their handlers are the first to enter a building when a bomb is suspected. Not even the bomb squad, who are specialists in removing and dismantling explosives, go before them. The K-9 team does not wear protective clothing while searching for bombs because no special suits could truly protect them. The work is that dangerous.

A handler's primary concern is for the safety of his canine, so he surveys the area before he allows his

Cassie, a 2-year-old Labrador retriever, sits among inactive explosives at a military explosive disposal shop.

dog to proceed. The police officer might check for poisonous liquids on the floor, bits of broken glass, or holes in the floor.

Then, the handler and his K-9 begin the search. Officer Burger teaches his trainees to work the dogs from left to right, so they can keep track of which places have been checked. If the area is especially large, the officer mentally divides the room into smaller sections, or grids, to make the search more manageable.

The dog is given the command "check," and he begins to sniff for explosive scents. The canine and his handler search the area carefully. The dog smells for bombs in air vents and around electrical outlets. Although the team needs to be thorough, they must also work quickly because a bomb may explode at any second.

The handler knows how to read his canine's behavior during a bomb search. When a K-9 is sensing explosives, his breathing often becomes faster and his nostrils open wider to capture more air and additional scent. Some dogs hold their tails and ears differently when they detect an explosive smell. When the officer notices these changes in his dog, he inspects that section for any physical evidence of a bomb.

If there's evidence of an explosive, or the dog silently alerts to explosive scent, the K-9 unit exits the building. Then, they provide the bomb squad with the bomb's exact location.

Tracking Down Narcotics

Police officers arrive at the apartment of an illegal drug dealer. A **narcotics** detection dog accompanies one of the officers. The officer unleashes the K-9, and tells him to search for illegal drugs. The dog sniffs for the scent of narcotics throughout the home. Within moments, the dog scratches furiously at a suitcase in the closet. The K-9 handler opens the luggage, finds numerous packages of cocaine, and arrests the drug dealer.

A narcotics detection dog is trained to find illegal drugs by using his sharp sense of smell. The Dutchess County Sheriff's Office trains some of their German shepherd patrol dogs as narcotics detectors. However, other breeds with keen scenting abilities, such as Labrador retrievers, are often used by police agencies for detection work.

To train dogs to sniff out drugs, the officer and the K-9 attend a 6-week narcotics detection school. The dog and officer team learn to find marijuana, hashish, cocaine, crack cocaine, heroin, methamphetamines, and ecstasy.

Each dog arrives at the school with a favorite toy, perhaps a towel or a small length of fire hose. At first, a bit of a single narcotic is placed inside the toy, and the officer and his dog play tug of war with the scented toy. Through this exercise, the dog is learning how the drug smells.

Next, the toy containing the narcotic's scent is hidden. The K-9 handler commands the dog to find the drugs, and he begins to sniff. Because the odor of narcotics travels through the air, the K-9 air scents to locate the toy. When he finds the plaything, the dog enjoys a rousing tug game with his handler, and gets plenty of praise.

To indicate that the dog has found narcotics, the K-9 learns to scratch or bark, which is known as an active or aggressive alert. The dogs learn to alert in this way

A narcotics detection dog is trained to find illegal drugs by using his sharp sense of smell. These K-9s learn to find various drugs, including cocaine.

by training on a scratchboard. This piece of equipment has wooden sides and a piece of transparent Plexiglas on the top. The dog's toy is attached to a rope, so it can be pulled from side to side under the Plexiglas. The dog is encouraged to scratch at the spot on the Plexiglas directly above his toy.

During the final step of narcotics detection schooling, the instructor hides an amount of the illegal drug, and then orders the dog to locate it. When the dog finds the narcotics, his handler throws the favorite toy to the exact area where the

To indicate the presence of narcotics, dogs learn to scratch or bark, which is known as an active or aggressive alert. This dog is sniffing for drugs that may be hidden in school lockers.

drugs were hidden. The dog makes this connection: *Wow! I find the drugs, my toy suddenly appears, and it's time for fun!*

UP FOR A CHALLENGE

Narcotics detection dogs continue to train long after graduating detection school. Groups of handlers and their detection K-9s meet for frequent training sessions. They practice in various locations, such as warehouses or motels, to challenge the dogs to work in different environments.

During a motel training exercise, for example, the trainer may hide illegal drugs in a motel room. He might tuck the narcotics high on a closet shelf or in a bathtub drain. Then, the canine handler and the dog are called into the room.

First, the handler checks the area for anything that could harm his dog. He looks for any open packages of narcotics. If the dog eats even a small amount of cocaine or heroin, it could die. The police officer also inspects the room for drug equipment, items such as razor blades or needles. When all appears safe, the dog is unhooked from the leash and commanded to find the drugs.

The police officer understands air currents and how they affect the scent of narcotics. The officer will make note of drafty sliding glass doors in the room or of an air conditioning vent and predict how these elements might move the scent around.

Working as a team, the handler stays close to the dog as it searches for narcotics. The handler has learned to read his particular dog's behavior. He will know, for example, that his dog breathes more quickly or keeps his tail in the air when he detects the scent of illegal drugs.

To further challenge the K-9 team, the trainer will vary the amount of narcotics that is hidden. One

PSEUDO-SCENTS

If a narcotics detection dog eats even a bit of certain illegal drugs, like cocaine or heroin, the K-9 could die. With this concern in mind, some police officers choose to use pseudo-scents during early narcotics detection training. Pseudo-scents are chemicals manufactured to smell like particular narcotics, yet they don't pose a deadly hazard to the dogs. Pseudo-scents may be used in place of real narcotics to scent the dog's toy during initial training.

Police officers who decide to use pseudo-scents in narcotics detection training quickly advance to using the actual narcotics scents. When a police officer testifies in court about the dog's drug finds, the testimony is more convincing if he can say that his dog was trained on real narcotics' scent.

A handful of chemical companies formulate pseudo-scents. They produce narcotics pseudo-scents that can be substituted for the real thing. They may also make scents that could be used in training cadaver detection dogs or search and rescue dogs. These pseudo-scents include the smell of human remains, the scent of a drowned body, and the odor of a human being in distress.

time, he might place a large quantity of marijuana in a dresser drawer. In another instance, he might take a pinch of cocaine and slide it underneath a chair cushion. The dog needs to alert his handler to an overwhelming narcotic scent, as well as to a vague smell of illegal drugs.

During training, it's a bonus if the motel room has recently had a canine guest. Narcotics detection dogs need to ignore the odor of other dogs and concentrate on the work at hand. Many drug dealers own aggressive dogs, so detecting drugs despite the presence of pet smells is a vital skill for the narcotics detection K-9.

Narcotic detection work is riddled with dangers. Drug dealers can be armed and violent, and their dogs are often trained to attack. Plus, because drugs are hazardous to police dogs, handlers must carry a remedy in case a dog accidentally ingests narcotics.

The narcotics detection team risks personal safety and toils long hours to be certain the community streets remain free of illegal drugs.

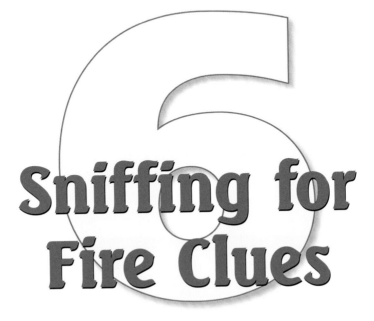

Sniffing for Fire Clues

Flames shoot high above a home, and firefighters arrive to bring the fire under control. Much of the house and its contents are burned, but fortunately, nobody is injured. The Dutchess County Fire Investigation Team in New York State believes an arsonist, a criminal who deliberately sets fires, might have started the blaze.

The Fire Investigation Team contacts Dutchess County Sheriff's Office Lieutenant Charles Hicks and his golden retriever, Timber. Timber is an accelerant detection dog. He is trained to use his sense of smell to locate **accelerants**, which are substances used to quicken the pace of a fire. Lt. Hicks and Timber will help the Fire Investigation Team gather evidence from the fire scene.

Lt. Hicks found Timber through a golden retriever rescue organization. These groups save golden retrievers from animal shelters across the country and match the dogs with caring owners. Timber was 2½ years old when he partnered with Lt. Hicks.

Lieutenant Charles Hicks and his accelerant detection dog, Timber, demonstrate how dogs can locate substances that may be used to quicken the pace of a fire. Timber can identify more than two dozen accelerants.

Lt. Hicks knew that Labradors and golden retrievers make good accelerant detection dogs. They have calm personalities and can stay relaxed and focused at a busy fire scene.

Lt. Hicks and Timber attended the New York State Fire Academy to learn accelerant detection. The schooling is similar to that of narcotics detection. A few drops of a single accelerant were placed inside Timber's special towel toy, and he and Lt. Hicks played with the towel. Then, the scented towel was hidden, and Timber was commanded to find the accelerant scent. Finally, just the accelerant scent was hidden for Timber to locate. Unlike narcotics detection dogs, Timber learned to sit, giving a passive alert, when he detected accelerants.

By the end of accelerant school, Timber could identify 26 different accelerant scents, including gasoline, kerosene, and rubbing alcohol.

WORKING THE FIRE SCENE

At the scene of a fire, Lt. Hicks first makes certain that the surroundings are free of dangers to Timber. Then, he releases Timber and has the dog search for accelerants. When Timber sits, evidence is gathered from that spot, placed in an evidence collection container, and sent to a laboratory to be checked. The laboratory experts determine what type of accelerant is present in the sample.

An accelerant detector dog uses its keen nose to help search for accelerants at a fire scene. Handlers use these dogs' finds to put the pieces of the fire scene puzzle together.

Timber is a valuable member of the fire investigation team. His ability to detect accelerants reduces the number of samples the team would normally collect by one-half. Not only does Timber save time and effort for the team, but he also saves money. Each of the evidence samples costs hundreds of dollars for the laboratory personnel to test. It saves the department about half their cost when Timber is called to the scene.

Lt. Hicks and Timber work as a team at the fire site. Timber uses his keen nose to uncover accelerants, and Lt. Hicks utilizes his keen police sense to put the pieces of the fire scene puzzle together. For example, Timber alerts in the home's bathroom. Lt. Hicks knows that nail polish remover, an accelerant, would normally be found in that room of the house. Lt. Hicks decides that the arsonist probably did not set the fire using the nail polish remover that Timber detected.

Outside the fire-damaged house, Timber makes his rounds to detect possible suspects. Arsonists are known for hanging around the fire scene to watch their criminal handiwork. When arsonists start fires, they use large amounts of accelerant and sometimes mistakenly splash the chemicals on their bodies and clothes. Lt. Hicks walks Timber through the crowd of onlookers at the scene, and Timber quietly sniffs the people for hints of accelerants. If Timber alerts near a particular person, the police can question that individual. When there are several arson suspects, the officers put the people in a lineup. Then, Timber can use his scenting skills to narrow down the suspects to the one who smells of accelerants.

TRAINING TIMBER

Beyond work at the fire sites, Timber and Lt. Hicks attend monthly detector training. There, Timber's

GOLDEN K-9S

Golden retrievers were once bred to hunt birds, especially waterfowl, such as ducks and geese. The breed was historically trained to enter a body of water to bring back birds that a hunter had shot. When people think of police dogs, golden retrievers don't necessarily come to mind, but this breed's intelligence and keen sense of smell make it a hard-working K-9. These dogs are known to have calm personalities, so police departments often showcase their golden retriever K-9s to enable families to have an up-close look at how police dogs work.

Golden retrievers were originally bred as waterfowl hunting dogs, but they can make good K-9 police dogs.

Not all golden retrievers are trained young to be police dogs. Nick is a golden retriever who works for the West Virginia Division of Corrections K-9 unit. This boisterous, active dog was once a family pet, but he became too unruly and too big for his family to handle. He bounced around from foster home to foster home because families couldn't control the high-energy dog. One day, Nick—who at the time was called Scooby—caught the attention of West Virginia's K-9 unit. They decided to try him out for police work, putting him through a tough 13-week training session. Nick successfully completed police dog training, and he now uses his hard-earned skills to help police officers find illegal drugs in prisons.

nose is given a workout. In one instance, a trainer placed one drop of accelerant on a gum wrapper, wadded the paper into a tiny ball, and threw it on the floor of a warehouse for Timber to find. Another time, the trainer slipped a cotton ball scented with accelerant into the pocket of a raincoat and hung the coat on a rack with other clothes. Timber sat right next to the coat with his nose pointing toward the pocket. Training like this helps keep Timber's accelerant detection skills in tip-top shape.

Timber is not the only one who requires training challenges. Lt. Hicks faces handler challenges, as well. During one session, the instructor hid a scented item in a room. The dogs each passed that room and ran down a long hallway. Why weren't the dogs catching the scent?

Lt. Hicks and the other K-9 handlers realized that the building was designed for a company that assembled computers. Because the company didn't want any particles to land on their delicate computer chips, the rooms were equipped with sealed doors and a ventilation system to keep the dust and dirt out. The handlers discovered that the scent was being pushed out to the end of the hallway, exactly where the dogs were detecting it!

Bloodhounds: The Scent Trailers

A young child wanders away from home in the middle of the night. Her parents are sound asleep and no one realizes she is missing until the morning. Her parents frantically search the neighborhood. When they can't find her, they telephone the police.

In cases like these, police officers may ask for the help of a bloodhound and its handler. Often, the bloodhound is requested when a scent trail is old. Bloodhounds are known for following aged scent trails that can be days old. These dogs are also useful

Bloodhounds are especially good at following, or trailing, a particular person's scent. Police officers often ask for the help of a bloodhound during missing-person cases.

when many people, such as the child's parents, have been walking around the area and contaminating the trail with their scent. Bloodhounds trail one specific person's scent and can ignore everyone else's odor.

At the youngster's home, the bloodhound handler chooses a scent article containing the child's scent, such as a mitten. The handler must be certain that no other person has touched this item and left scent on it. The dog, wearing his harness and long lead, takes a whiff of the mitten. He instantly starts to trail the girl's scent, locating her in a rather short time.

OUTSTANDING POLICE DOGS

Formal police dog training first took place in Belgium and Germany in the early 1900s. Since then, police K-9s have played a major part in protecting communities. Throughout history, many police dogs have gained special recognition for their work. Big or small, when it comes to police dogs, every K-9 has an amazing story.

Midge, a 6-pound Chihuahua-rat terrier mix, is just beginning her police dog career. Yet she has already made national news. Midge is partnered with Sheriff Daniel McClelland of the Geauga County Sheriff's Office in Ohio and certified in marijuana detection. Because she is so tiny, she can search for drugs in the small confines of a vehicle or in tight spaces.

Bruno, a German shepherd, was bred by Guiding Eyes for the Blind in New York, but he took a different work path. Instead

(continues)

Midge, a 6-pound Chihuahua-rat terrier mix, gets along with another drug-sniffing police K-9 in her unit, Brutus.

(continued)

of becoming a guide dog, Bruno joined the East Hartford Police Department in Connecticut. During his career, Bruno and his partner Police Officer William Proulx arrested 1,100 criminals, and found nine lost children and three Alzheimer's patients. Bruno received the 1994 Daniel Wasson Memorial K-9 Award, given by the Connecticut Police Work Dog Association, because he helped his police partner disarm an assailant.

Police Officer Humberto Morales and his German shepherd partner, Niko, work for the New London Police Department in Connecticut. Niko was honored with two Daniel Wasson Awards for his heroic actions. In 2003, Niko tracked three robbery suspects into the woods. One of the criminals shot the K-9, but the dog didn't let that stop him from tracking them. The following year, Niko located a murderer in a pitch-black basement, and the criminal was arrested.

A bloodhound's specialty is man trailing, or following a particular person. When a bloodhound sniffs a scent article, it is gathering the smell of that person's skin rafts. The scent of a person's skin rafts smells only like that individual. As the bloodhound takes scent from the article, the dog detects other odors, too. For example, the dog will notice the odor of the toiletries the person uses, such as shampoos or soap, and the scent of the person's laundry detergent. Even the type of food a person has eaten helps form the individual's unique scent.

A bloodhound's body is specially designed for scent work. This dog's nostrils have extra long slits to allow a large amount of scent to enter. Plus, the dog has an estimated 220 million olfactory receptor cells, which are responsible for gathering scent. The folds in the dog's facial skin trap and hold scent close to its nose. The bloodhound's slobbery jowls moisten the scent, keeping it alive and strong. In addition, the dog's ears hang low, allowing them to drag on the ground when the dog is trailing and kick the scent up toward the dog's nose.

A bloodhound trails a person rather than tracking that individual. The dog does not follow an individual footstep by footstep; instead this dog seeks the strongest scent and pursues it. For example, if a criminal completely circled a tree before continuing, the experienced bloodhound wouldn't bother to go around the tree. The dog would just trail in a straight line and catch up with the most recent scent.

THE YOUNG BLOODHOUND

Police Officer Mitch Serlin, of the Westchester County Police Department in New York State, is the handler of a female bloodhound named Gracie. Officer Serlin found Gracie through a bloodhound rescue organization.

Officer Serlin wanted a dog that was independent, not one that relied on the pack. A bloodhound must lead on the trail and not look back at the handler for reassurance or direction. The officer also needed a dog that wanted to look for people. He tested Gracie's hunt drive by hiding to see if she would try to find him. "If the dog likes to play hide and seek, she has a hunt drive," he explains.

Once he chose young Gracie, Officer Serlin began training. Teaching the bloodhounds differs from training other K-9s. Bloodhounds are not taught many obedience commands. The dogs must be confident enough to lead on the trail and not wait for orders from the handler.

In addition, typical K-9 obedience training uses a tug on the leash as correction for unacceptable behavior. However, the bloodhound's training does not involve such corrections. Imagine that a bloodhound handler races behind his bloodhound on a treacherous wilderness trail, and the handler trips. As he falls, he accidentally tugs on the lead. If the bloodhound had been taught with leash corrections, the dog would think it had done something wrong and stop trailing. A bloodhound handler doesn't want his dog to stop when the canine has the scent.

Trailing is a bloodhound's extraordinary skill, so it is the focus of the dog's training. Bloodhound handlers work every day to help make their K-9s superior trailing dogs.

8
Scent Trailers Learn to Trail

How does a police officer teach a bloodhound to trail? Bryan Corns is a New York State Police Trooper and handler of Otis, a bloodhound. Trooper Corns explains that bloodhounds are born with the ability to follow scent. The handler's job is to challenge the dog's inborn trailing know-how.

At first, Trooper Corns grabbed a dog biscuit and hid in the short grass about 15 feet away from Otis. Another trainer held Otis until Trooper Corns was hidden; then, the dog was instructed to find his handler. Otis loved to find Trooper Corns because he was rewarded with the dog biscuit. Bloodhounds are big fans of food, so treats are often given as rewards at the end of a successful trail. The goodies aren't always dog food either. Westchester County Police Officer Serlin awards his bloodhound, Gracie, with a slice or two of pepperoni when she finishes her trails.

For the next step in training, Trooper Corns traded places with the other trainer and had him hide. Otis learned to locate the other trainer. Because a bloodhound's job is to find strangers, the dog needs to learn to search for people other than its handler.

The use of a scent article is also introduced in a bloodhound's early training. The trainer who was going to hide would drop an article, such as a hat, for Otis to sniff. That way, the trainer taught the dog

Bloodhound Otis works with his police partner, New York State Police Trooper Bryan Corns, to trail criminals and find missing people. Otis focuses his full attention on tracing a scent when necessary.

that the scent on the object matched the scent of the person he needed to find.

Gradually, the scent trails laid for Otis became longer, had more turns, and were in more heavily wooded areas. Trooper Corns also increased the time between laying the scent trails and having Otis follow them. In the beginning, Otis trained on trails that were about one hour old. He advanced to trails that were 24 hours old.

At the end of every trail, the person who laid the trail was waiting for the dog. Bloodhounds sniff the discovered person to be sure he or she is the one the dog has been trailing. The bloodhound then jumps up on the individual to confirm that the person is the one the dog was seeking.

Luckily, trained bloodhounds aren't usually aggressive. Dutchess County Sheriff's Office Deputy Carl Merritt, handler of bloodhound Barney, says that a person found by Barney doesn't need to be afraid of the dog. A bloodhound is more likely to lick the individual than to bite. Don't let a bloodhound's calm demeanor fool you, though. If someone threatened Deputy Merritt, Barney would act aggressively to protect his handler.

GOING TO COURT

A bloodhound's positive identification of the sought-after person plays an especially important part in a criminal investigation. Let's say that Otis and Trooper Corns are called to a burglarized home. The burglar had rifled through a dresser drawer and had dropped an item to the floor. If no one else has touched the object, it can be used as a scent article for Otis to sniff.

Otis and Trooper Corns trail the burglar through twists and turns, until Otis finds the criminal and places his front paws on the lawbreaker. Because Otis is a purebred bloodhound, his identification of the man as the burglar is admissible as evidence in court in 47 states.

Of course, Otis can't take the witness stand, so Trooper Corns testifies in court about the trailing work that led to the burglar. He brings a fat folder filled with written accounts of Otis' trailing exploits. These papers are proof that Otis is a well-trained and reliable man trailer.

TRICKY TRAILS

Officer Serlin and Gracie often train with Deputy Merritt and Barney. It can be confusing to the dog for his own handler to lay a scent trail for him. The bloodhound realizes the scent he is tracking belongs to the guy holding the lead, so the dog keeps looking back. For this reason, each officer will lay a scent trail for the other's bloodhound.

When Officer Serlin lays a trail, he might race around telephone poles, into the woods, and through

THE BEAGLE BRIGADE

A descendent of the bloodhound, the beagle, is used as a detector dog for the United States Department of Agriculture's Animal and Plant Health Inspection Services. The USDA calls their dogs on duty the Beagle Brigade. The beagles detect prohibited fruits, plants, and meats to keep them from entering the United States. These goods might contain insects, such as the Mediterranean fruit fly, or diseases, such as foot and mouth disease, which could threaten the U.S. food supply. The beagles sniff luggage and other containers at international airports to find the restricted food.

Beagles were specially chosen for this job because of their keen sense of smell and natural curiosity. These dogs love food, which helps them perform their food-finding duties. Beagles are also small and friendly, so they can sniff baggage without bothering the airport crowds.

(continues)

Ilka Mathis and Comet are part of the USDA's Beagle Brigade, checking luggage at international airports for prohibited or restricted foods or plants.

(continued)

The beagles that join the program might be donated by private citizens, bought from breeders, or adopted from an animal shelter. The dogs attend an 8 to 12 week training program at the USDA National Detector Dog Training Center in Orlando, Florida.

At the training center, the dogs learn to give a passive alert, or to sit, when they detect the scent of citrus fruit, mango, apple, beef, or pork. Each beagle is presented with a group of boxes. When a dog alerts someone to the box containing the proper odor, it is rewarded with food. Beagles learn more food scents throughout their working years. Some of the beagles in the brigade can detect more than 50 different food odors!

streams to challenge Deputy Merritt and Barney. Many people think that a criminal could lose a bloodhound if the individual ran through water. However, bloodhounds can catch the person's scent on the other side of the streambed, where the scent clings to the bank.

Deputy Merritt has an idea to really test Gracie's nose. He is planning a trail where he will climb one tree and swing to another without letting his feet touch the ground. Deputy Merritt wants to see if Gracie can still detect and follow his scent.

Officer Serlin and Gracie welcome such difficult trails. Once in a while, he has someone lay a scent trail through an amusement park near his home.

Then, he and Gracie will find that very person among the thousands of visitors at the park.

For another challenge, Officer Serlin might have a person enter a high-rise building. The person will take the elevator to an upper floor, leave the elevator, and hide in an office. He and Gracie will hop on the elevator and stop at each floor until she catches the person's scent.

During these practice sessions, each officer learns to read his dog's trailing behavior. Most bloodhounds have their noses down and tails up while they have the scent. They also keep a constant pull on the lead when they are successfully trailing.

The officers run trails with their bloodhounds during the day and at night. They trail in all types of weather because the team must learn how air currents and weather conditions affect scent. Usually, moist conditions allow the scent to stay strong. On the other hand, hot weather can bake the skin rafts, so little scent is present.

Like all K-9 handlers, bloodhound handlers are responsible for their dogs' safety. Keeping trained bloodhounds safe is a bit of a challenge because these dogs are so focused on scenting that they often don't see the objects in front of them. Officer Serlin has had to prevent Gracie from crashing into wire fences. Otis has the same type of difficulty, confides Trooper Corns. "When Otis is trailing, he might walk into a wall," he says.

Police K-9s are highly trained dogs that have the expertise to help police officers perform important duties.

If you ever see a bloodhound bump into something, the dog is probably hot on a trail. The bloodhound and his handler might be close to catching a criminal or locating a lost child. The bloodhound teams, as well as every police dog and handler that are called to duty, work hard to make the community a secure place to live.

Like their human police counterparts, dogs that engage in police work should be respected for their hard work and expertise. Thanks to these brave and persistent K-9s, police officers can more easily find evidence, criminals, or even missing people. Police dogs play a vital role in keeping our towns, cities, and states safe places to live.

Glossary

Accelerants substances used to quicken the pace of a fire

Agility the ability to move quickly and gracefully

Air scenting a K-9's act of following a specific scent through the air

Cadavar a dead body

Decoy someone or something used to draw attention

Narcotics addictive drugs that can change a person's mood and reduce pain; many are illegal

Olfactory sensory cells sensory structures that allow the dog to detect scent

Rafts dead skin cells that float on air currents and have a particular odor that a canine can detect and follow

Shutzhund a dog sport that includes tracking, obedience, and protection work

Temperament the natural mental, physical and emotional traits of an animal

Tracking line a long leash the handler attaches to a K-9 for tracking or trailing

Bibliography

Albrecht, Kat and Jana Murphy. *The Lost Pet Chronicles.* New York: Bloomsbury, 2004.

Ashworth, James (Village of Wappingers Falls Police Department, Police Officer, K-9 Handler). Interview with the author, Poughkeepsie, New York, February 24, 2005.

Burger, Mike (Town of Poughkeepsie, Police Officer, K-9 Trainer and Handler). Interview with the author, Fishkill, New York, January 27, 2005.

Christman, Dan (New York City Department of Environmental Protection Police, Police Officer, K-9 Handler). Interview with the author, Poughkeepsie, New York, February 3, 2005.

Corns, Bryan (New York State Police, Trooper, Bloodhound Handler). Interview with the author, Rhinebeck, New York, August 27, 2005.

Dahlem, Joseph (Dutchess County Sheriff's Office, Deputy, K-9 Handler). Interview with the author, Pleasant Valley, New York, February 3, 2005.

"Frequently Asked Questions About Belgian Malinois." American Belgian Malinois Club. Available online. URL: www.breedclub.org/malfaq.htm.

Gorrell, Gena K. *Working Like A Dog.* Toronto, Ontario: Tundra, 2003.

Hicks, Charles (Dutchess County Sheriff's Office, Lt., K-9 Trainer and Handler). Interviews with the author, Fishkill, New York, January 27, 2005. Poughkeepsie, New York, February 3, 2005, Poughkeepsie, New York, February 24, 2005, Rhinebeck, New York, August 27, 2005.

"ID a Malinois." American Belgian Malinois Rescue. Available online. URL: www.malinoisrescue.org/abmcidmal.shtml

Jackson, Donna M. *Hero Dogs: Courageous Canines in Action*. New York: Megan Tingley Books, 2003.

Jonas, Timothy, and Ernie Bueker. "Accelerant Detection Canines." United States Police Canine Association. Available online. URL: http://uspcak9.com/training/accelerant.shtml

Keystone Golden Retriever Rescue, Inc. "Nick the Narcotics Officer." Available online. URL: http://www.kgrrescue.com/placements.htm

Kilpatrick, Kelly (New York City Department of Environmental Protection Police, Police Officer, K-9 Handler). Interview with the author, Fishkill, New York, January 27, 2005.

LaMonica, Frank (Dutchess County Sheriff's Office, Sergeant, K-9 Trainer, and Handler). Interviews with the author, Salt Point, New York, June 10, 2004, Fishkill, New York, January 27, 2005, Poughkeepsie, New York, February 24, 2005, Rhinebeck, New York, August 27, 2005.

Marinelli, Greg (New York City Department of Environmental Protection Police, Police Officer, K-9 Handler). Interviews with the author, Fishkill, New York, January 27, 2005, Poughkeepsie, New York, February 3, 2005, Poughkeepsie, New York, February 24, 2005.

McClelland, Daniel (Geauga County Sheriff's Office, Sheriff, K-9 Handler) Telephone interview with the author, November 20, 2006.

McKay, Bill (Dutchess County Sheriff's Office, Deputy, K-9 Handler). Interview with the author, Pleasant Valley, New York, March 21, 2005.

Merritt, Carl (Dutchess County Sheriff's Office, Deputy, Bloodhound Handler). Interview with the author, Poughkeepsie, New York, February 3, 2005.

Presnall, Judith Janda. *Police Dogs.* San Diego, CA: Kidhaven Press, 2002.

Russell, Joan Plummer. *Aero and Officer Mike: Police Partners.* Honesdale, PA: Boyds Mills Press, 2001.

Serlin, Mitch (Westchester County Police Department, Police Officer, Bloodhound Handler). Interview with the author, Poughkeepsie, New York, February 3, 2005.

Syrotuck, William G. *Scent and the Scenting Dog.* Mechanicsburg, PA: Barkleigh Productions, Inc., 1972, reprint 2000.

The Daniel Wasson Memorial K-9 Award Previous Award Recipients. Connecticut Police Work Dog Association. Available online. URL: www.cpwds.com/wasson_award.htm.

"There's a New Dog in Town: The Beagle Brigade." *Customs and Border Protection Today.* April 2003. Available online. URL: http://www.cbp.gov/xp/CustomsToday/2003/April/new_dog.xml

Valkys, Michael. "More Dogs Sniffing Out Crime: Canines Aid Wider Variety of Cases" *Poughkeepsie Journal.* May 6, 2002. Available online. URL: http://www.poughkeepsiejournal.com/projects/crimebeat/po050602s2.shtml.

For More Information

Find out more about the training and work of the dogs in this book by contacting these organizations.

Bureau of Alcohol, Tobacco, Firearms, and Explosives
Canine Operations Branch
650 Massachusetts Ave. NW
Washington, DC 20226
202-927-8680
www.atf.gov

Dutchess County Sheriff's Office
150 N. Hamilton Street
Poughkeepsie, New York 12601-2011

National Police Bloodhound Association
www.npba.com

U.S. Customs and Border Protection
1300 Pennsylvania Ave.
Washington, DC 20229
www.cbp.gov

United States Police Canine Association
P.O. Box 80
Springboro, OH 45066
800-531-1614
www.uspcak9.com

Anderson, Bendix. *Security Dogs.* New York: Bearport Publishing Company, Inc., 2005.

Gorrell, Gena K. *Working Like a Dog.* Toronto, Ontario: Tundra, 2003.

Jackson, Donna M. *Hero Dogs: Courageous Canines in Action.* New York: Megan Tingley Books, 2003.

Presnall, Judith Janda. *Police Dogs.* San Diego, CA: Kidhaven Press, 2002.

Ruffin, Frances E. *Police Dogs.* New York: Bearport Publishing Company, Inc., 2005.

Russell, Joan Plummer. *Aero and Officer Mike: Police Partners.* Honesdale, PA: Boyds Mills Press, 2001.

Web Sites

Central Intelligence Agency
www.odci.gov/cia/ciakids/dogs/index.shtml
Learn about the training and work of the CIA K-9s.

City of Mountainview, California
http://www.ci.mtnview.ca.us/city_hall/police/about_us/k9.asp
Meet the police dogs of Mountainview.

Federal Bureau of Investigation
www.fbi.gov/kids/dogs/doghome.htm
Information about working dogs and the K-9s of the FBI.

North American Police Work Dog Association

http://www.napwda.com/tips/index.phtml

Read about valiant K-9s that gave their lives in the line of service.

Working Dog Foundation

www.workingdog.org/kidskorner.html

Police K-9 information with links to other useful sites.

Picture Credits

Index